Robin Hood

Illustrated by

GREG HILDEBRANDT

Adapted from the novel by

J. Walker McSpadden

The Unicorn Publishing House
New Jersey

I n the days of good King Harry the Second of England—he of the warring sons—there were certain forests in the north country set aside for the King's hunting, and no man might shoot a deer under penalty of death. These forests were well guarded by the King's Foresters, who were equal in authority in their wood as the Sheriff was in his walled town, or even to the Bishop in his abbey.

One of the largest of the royal forests was that of Sherwood and Barnesdale near the two towns of Nottingham and Barnesdale. Here lived a Head Forester, Hugh Fitzooth, with his wife and little son Robert. The boy had been born in Lockesley town, in the year 1160, and was often called Rob of Lockesley. He was a handsome boy, sturdy of frame, who loved to roam in the green forest or sit by the fire and listen to his father's woodland tales.

During the happy days of his childhood, Rob had two playmates, his cousin Will Gamewell and the child of the Earl of Huntingdon, Marion Fitzwalter. Rob's father and Marion's father were enemies of long standing. People whispered that Hugh Fitzooth was the rightful Earl and had been cheated of his land by Fitzwalter. Little did Rob and Marion care for their fathers' affairs, being content to roam the great greenwood together, smelling the sweet flowers and listening to the songbirds of the forest.

But the days of youth soon fled, and before long troubled skies gathered over the greenwood. Rob's father had other enemies too, namely the lean Sheriff of Nottingham and the fat Bishop of Hereford. By evil lies and trickery they convinced the King that Rob's father was an unjust man. Poor Hugh Fitzooth found himself removed from his post as King's Forester, and one cold winter's evening, the Sheriff came to arrest him for treason. Rob was but nineteen, helpless against the Sheriff's troops as they took his father away to prison.

Rob and his mother were taken into the home of their kinsman, Squire George of Gamewell, who though kind and generous as a man can possibly be, he could not remove the shock and loss that Rob's mother suffered. She died in two months, and Rob's father followed her soon after while in prison awaiting trial.

Two years passed by, and still Rob mourned the loss of his parents and the happy days. Marion had been sent to the court of Queen Eleanor and Will went to school, so Rob roamed the great greenwood alone. One morning Rob heard news of an archer's tournament to be held in Nottingham. More than glad to test his skill against other bowmen, Rob set off at once for the upcoming Fair.

As Rob passed through Sherwood Forest he chanced upon a group of Foresters. One glance told Robin he had found an enemy, for there was the man who took his father's place as Forester. They saw Rob and began to jest.

"How now! Where goes this pretty little lad with his tupenny bow and toy arrows?" roared the Head Forester with laughter.

"My bow is has good as yours and my arrows shoot just as true," Rob replied.

The Forester challenged Rob to shoot half the distance to a herd of the King's deer that grazed a full hundred yards away. Rob took the challenge, boasting he would drop the head stag. His arrow flew and found its mark as the deer leaped high into the air. The Forester was shocked, but turned to Rob in a rage and bade him to leave at once upon penalty of death for killing the King's deer.

As Rob turned to leave he spoke an oath against his old enemy, which prompted the Forester to return the thrust with a flying arrow at Rob's head. Luckily, the arrow just missed him, and turning about, he let loose a stinging reply. Straight flew his answering shaft, and with a cry the Forester fell dead. Though just cause brought him to kill, Rob was now branded as an outlaw. He took refuge at a friend's home in the forest. There he fell in with other men who had been unjustly accused.

They were in need of a brave man to lead their band, and offered Rob the chance to be their leader if he could win the tournament and secure the golden arrow.

Rob arrived at the tourney disguised as a common beggar, and lucky he did, for reward posters were everywhere calling for his capture. As he joined the line of other men ready to test their skill, Rob chanced to look up at the Sheriff's box that oversaw the Fair. Rob's heart leaped with joy as he cast his eye upon the fair features of Maid Marion. But he said nothing, only resolved himself all the more to win the golden arrow so that he might place it in her gentle hand.

The tournament was a fierce competition, with many skilled archers, but to the surprise and delight of the audience, a beggar ran away with it. The crowd cried, "a bull! a bull!" as Rob made the center mark again and again.

Rob took the golden arrow and presented to the lovely Maid Marion, who knew the brave man that stood before her. She accepted the arrow with a gentle touch of her hand and softly said, "Many thanks, Rob in the Hood."

The Sheriff was furious that a beggar had beat his best archers, and greater insult, that he had not given the arrow to his daughter. Fortunately, Rob disappeared before being set upon, and rejoining the band, became their leader. The merry band quickly gained fame as defenders of the poor and helpless, enemies to the wicked and unjust, and champions of the greenwood who had as their leader a man now known as Robin Hood.

By the following summer, Robin's band numbered eighty, all sworn to him and at his beckoning when once he blew his horn. One day, desiring excitement, Robin set out in search of adventure. Indeed, it wasn't long before he found more than he could handle.

Reaching a stream, he found a log foot-bridge by which he could make a crossing. But as he ventured onto the bridge, another chose to cross at that moment—a huge hulk of a man.

"Give way, fellow!" roared Robin.

"Nay," spoke the stranger, "I give way only to a better man

than myself."

"Give way, I say, or I'll show you a better man by dunking you soundly in this stream!"

At this challenge both men sought sound wooden staffs with which to do battle. When once again they came to the center of the bridge the battle was joined. "Have at you!" cried Robin, and the woods resounded with the thunder of their blows. Whack! whack! whack!

Robin managed for some time to elude the murderous blows of his opponent, until his footing slipped for just a moment and then *whack!* Robin's head filled with stars and he slipped neatly into the stream.

When he came to, the big stranger was over him, rendering what aid he could. Robin told him his name, which made the big fellow very sorry, for he had come to join the merry band, not to beat up their leader. But Robin gladly welcomed the newcomer, who called himself John Little, to which Robin replied he would now be known as Little John.

Little John became Robin's most trusted friend and companion, and would often accompany him on fine walks through the wood. On one bright morning, while the two were walking deep in the greenwood, they heard someone coming up the path ahead and whistling a happy tune. The two hid in the bushes to see who the stranger was, and before long, a dandy appeared.

"By my word, a gay bird!" whispered Robin, "let us lie still, and trust that his purse is not as light as his heart."

The stranger was finely dressed in scarlet and silk and wore a huge hat with a curling cock feather in it. As he approached, Robin stepped out in full view.

"Hold!" Robin said, "I am the tax gatherer of these woods and I bid you hand over your purse, sweet gentleman."

"You're a droll fellow," he replied calmly.

"If you don't give over your purse, I'll be forced to give you a sound drubbing."

"I think not, good fellow," he replied dryly.

"Hold, I say!" shouted Robin angerly; for he knew how Little

John must be chuckling at this from behind the bushes. "Hold I say, else I shall have to bloody those fair locks of yours!" And he swung his oak staff about to threaten the fellow.

"Alas!" moaned the stranger, shaking his head. "The pity of it all! Now I shall have to run this fellow through with my sword! And I hoped to be a peaceable man henceforth!" And sighing deeply he drew his shining blade and stood on guard.

"Put up your weapon," said Robin. "It is too pretty a piece of steel to be cracked by common oak; and that is what would happen on the first pass I made at you. Get a stick like mine and we will fight fairly, man to man."

The stranger thought a moment, eyeing Robin from head to foot, then went and laid hold of a good sound stick. The two fell to fighting at once, and Robin soon found a rude surprise. The dandy was incredibly strong and swift, and without much ado sent Robin tumbling to the ground. When the fight was over, the gentleman turned to Robin and said, "Do you not know your playmate of old, Will Gamewell!"

"Ha! Will! My old chum!" Robin cried.

They warmly embraced, and Will related that he had spent time with Maid Marion and she sent her love to Robin, though she could not be with him. Will told Robin he wished to join his band, to which Robin happily agreed, giving him the new name of Will Scarlet, because of his friend's fancy dress.

Summer arrived, and with it Robin's desire to test the metal of good men that might add to the strength of his band. Hearing of a friar that lived nearby who was by all reports one of the best bowman and swordsman in the land, Robin set out at once to find the man.

He came to a stream along the way and decided to rest awhile until he could think of a way to cross without getting wet. As he sat under a drooping willow he heard someone singing. Walking along the bank he came upon a fat friar preparing to eat a meat pie on the opposite side. With mischief in his heart, Robin drew an arrow to his bow and bid the good friar to cross the stream and carry him to the other side. The friar agreed to

Robin's request, not wishing to feel an arrow point, and carried Robin on his back.

Once across, the friar drew his sword before Robin could draw his, and then forced Robin to carry him. And if that wasn't enough, Robin got the jump again on the friar when they reached the shore, and tried to force the jolly fellow to carry him back. But this time Robin could not hold on to the big shoulders of the friar and fell right in the middle of the stream. Finally, they fell to swordplay, but after an hour neither of them had gained an advantage. Robin, realizing this was the same friar he was seeking, begged the fight cease and that they be friends. The monk was known as Friar Tuck, and when Robin told him his name and asked him to join his band, he could now count on one more worthy man to stand by his side.

That very evening, with a good supper under his belt, Robin set out for a woodland stroll. He had not gone far when he heard the sound of sweet music. He did not desire a fight that evening and wished to hear the song of the stranger, so he hid behind a tree and watched the fellow pass.

The singer was a sturdy yeoman, clad in scarlet, like Will, though he did not look quite as fine a gentleman. He had a sweeter voice though, and thrummed a harp as he walked along. His voice rang out this song:

> "Hey down, and a down, and a down!
> I've a lassie back i' the town;
> Come day, come night,
> Come dark or light,
> She will wed me, back i' the town!"

Robin let the singer pass, for the carols reminded him of his Maid Marion. When he returned to camp, he told his men to be on the lookout for the lover and if they chanced to see him, to bring the young man to him.

The very next day Little John and Much the miller's son found the young man, but though he carried his harp, he did

not use it. The fellow seemed to walk in sadness. They told him that Robin wished to speak with him.

When he arrived, he told Robin that his true love was to be given in marriage to a very old knight. The knight desired the land the girl had inherited, and struck a bargain with her brother. They were to be wed at three o'clock that day by the Bishop of Hereford.

Robin would not stand still for such trickery, and quickly devised a scheme to upset the old knight's wedding plans. He instructed Will to gather four-and-twenty bowman and meet him at the church, and bid Friar Tuck to leave immediately, for he would perform a marriage of love that day.

Robin arrived at the church disguised as a minstrel and told the fat Bishop that he would harp beautiful music for the married couple and bring them luck. Thereby Robin was able to send word of her lover, Allen-a-Dale, that all would be well. When the time came, Robin disavowed the marriage and blew his horn to call his bowman to take command. The maiden chose her lover, and kneeling before Friar Tuck, the couple exchanged their vows.

Now the Bishop had been locked up in the organ-loft of the church and the old knight was forced to perch at the top of a high tree, and both remained there all night till the people were sure Robin's band had gone.

So the two were understandably outraged and went straight to the Sheriff to demand he raise his troops to capture Robin and his band at once. The Sheriff entered Sherwood Forest with a hundred men, and finding a small hunting party, they surrounded and took captive the widow's three sons.

The widow appealed to Robin to help free her sons from the hangman's noose, and Robin, not about to let his dear friends die in such disgrace, devised a plan. Robin dressed as a poor beggar and entered Nottingham the morning of the executions.

With him, hidden in the crowd, were eighty of his best men. People had come from all parts to see the hanging, so many that it began to look like a day at the Fair. Robin, finding that

a man was yet to selected as hangman, approached the Sheriff and said, "Good sir, what will you give a silly old man today to be your hangman?"

The Sheriff looked over the haggard fellow before him and offered new clothes and thirteen pence for the job. Robin agreed and was led to the prisoners.

But when Robin led the sons to the gallows, he pulled off his rags and cried, "A rescue!"

Robin's men appeared from everywhere and quickly routed the Sheriff's troops, sending them running to avoid the sting of their arrows. Will Scarlet and Allen-a-Dale had overcome the guards at the town-gate, and Robin with his merry band made a clean escape back to the safety of the greenwood.

Now one day not long thereafter, Robin decided to try his skill at hunting and setoff into the greenwood. Presently a beautiful deer appeared in a glade and Robin drew his bow. But before he could let his arrow fly, the beast fell, pierced through the heart by a clever arrow from across the glade. In the next instant, a handsome little page appeared with bow in hand, over the slain animal.

Robin approached from the other side.

"How dare you shoot the King's beasts, stripling?" he asked severely.

"I have as much right as the King himself," said the page haughtily. "How dare you question me?"

Robin swore he knew that voice from the old days. "Who are you, my lad?" Robin said more kindly.

"No lad of yours, and my name's my own," replied the page.

"Softly! or we of the forest will teach you manners!" said Robin.

"Come, draw and defend yourself!" And the page drew his sword.

Robin was a bit amused at the notion of the little page challenging him, but decided to engage the lad in the sport. The bout lasted some quarter-hour and the page proved his skill with many a pretty fencing trick. But Robin with his supe-

rior strength soon wore down his opponent, and decided to let the lad prick his wrist to end the fight.

"Are you satisfied, fellow?" asked the page.

"Aye, and now can you tell to whom I owe this scratch?"

"I am Richard Partington, page to Her Majesty, Queen Eleanor," replied the other. "And though you might well be one of the King's men, know that I seek one Robin Hood, the outlaw, to whom I bring amnesty from the Queen. Do you know where he might be?"

Robin was about to answer when he caught sight of the arrow that had killed the deer, a golden arrow, and he knew it could be from no other.

"Ah! I know you now! By sight of yon golden arrow, on which I bestowed to thee at the Sheriff's tourney, you are Maid Marion!"

"Robin!" gasped Marion, for it was she.

Robin pushed the hood back from her face, then clasped the dainty page close to his breast and she in turn yielded right willingly.

Robin took Marion back with him to the wild wood where his merry band was waiting. A great feast took place and Marion related the wishes of her Queen. She bid Robin and four of his best archers travel to London and be in the next tournament. King Harry's best men would be shooting, and it would please the Queen to upstage her husband, for he had become quite vain about his men. In return, the Queen would grant Robin and his men full amnesty. Marion gave him a ring from Her Majesty as a show of good faith.

The morning of the great archery contest dawned fair and bright, bringing every citizen of London and the surrounding countryside to Finsbury Field, where the tourney would be held. Circling the field were the tent pavilions of the men-at-arms, each with its multi-colored pennant.

Suddenly the gates at the far end of the tents opened wide, and the populace rose in a mighty cheer. King Harry had arrived. He rode a fine white charger and was clad in a rich suit of velvet and satin. At his side rode Queen Eleanor, looking

regal and charming upon her sleek mare. The company dismounted and ascended the steps of the royal box.

The contest began, and though all who shot that day had excellent marks, it was the knight, Tepus, who scored no less than six center hits, easily winning the tourney. The King then opened the contest to all men, with the winner to be given the title of best archer in all England. A dozen men stepped forth and entered their names against the King's men.

"By my word!" said the King, "these must be hardy men to stand against my archers!"

"Think you the best archers in all of England, my lord?" asked the Queen.

"Aye, and in all the world besides," answered the King.

"I am inclined to make a wager," replied the Queen. "What if I could produce five archers who would out-shoot your best men, will you grant them full grace and amnesty?"

"Assuredly! Against five-hundred pounds," said the King in good humor.

The Queen accepted both the King's wager and one from the Bishop of Hereford. The contest continued, with the King's men easily beating all challengers in the open target match. But the question flew among the crowd, "Who would be the Queen's champions?"

The answer soon came as five men entered the gate, one dressed in scarlet and the others in suits of Lincoln green. The Bishop gasped and cried, "'Tis Robin Hood, the outlaw!"

The crowd went wild with excitement, and though a heavy frown cast upon the King's face, he would not break his promise of amnesty he made to his Queen. He granted Robin a forty day pardon and ordered the contest to begin.

Each man shot three arrows at an open target, and this time it was Gilbert of the White Hand who made the center mark every time. But Robin was the last to shoot, and boldly drew his bow back to let loose a shaft, then another, and another, without hardly a pause to check his mark.

Robin said to Gilbert, "You are worthy of being shot against,

and if you had but placed the arrows so, perhaps the King would declare you the best bowman in all England."

The onlookers were stunned, for Robin had placed his first two arrows just left of the center mark, side by side, and with the third arrow he spilt down between them, taking half of each, so from a distance all three looked like one immense arrow.

"Verily, I think your bow is armed with witchcraft!" cried Gilbert, but he could hardly be heard over the thunderous applause of the crowd.

The King departed in a great wrath, but never an ill word he said to his dear Queen. The Queen thanked Robin and his men and gave her blessing that they be safe, then departed with her ladies in waiting. Triumphant, Robin and his men returned to the greenwood.

The King kept his word and no harm befell Robin along the journey back to Sherwood Forest. However, the Sheriff received the royal word, that if he valued his office, he would lay hold of the outlaws without further delay. Indeed, Robin's exploits were now known throughout England, and the Sheriff was finding himself the butt of many a tavern joke for his failure to capture the outlaws.

But three expeditions into the greenwood brought nothing, prompting the Sheriff's daughter to scold her father, "A force of arms against Robin will never meet with success, but might we not meet his tricks with other tricks of our own?"

"Agreed," said the Sheriff. "Have you a plan in mind, my daughter?"

"No," she replied, "but I will think on it."

The very next day a braggart named Middle, a tinker by trade, appeared at the Sheriff's doorway looking for work. The Sheriff's daughter hit upon a scheme, that this simple fellow might undo Robin through his very simplicity. She gave him an arrest warrant and bid him find and capture the outlaw.

Along the road to Barnesdale the tinker met up with a young fellow with curling brown hair and merry eyes. "Good-day to you," said the young man.

"Good-day to you!" replied the tinker. "Whence come you, and know you any news?"

"Nay, nothing worthy to tell. What news have you?" asked the man.

"All I have to tell," said the tinker, puffing up in great pride, "is that I am especially commissioned to bring the outlaw Robin Hood to justice. Are you of a mind to aid me in this bold venture."

"Aye," said the stranger with a roguish grin, "but let us retire to the tavern where we can make a plan in greater comfort."

At the inn the tinker took heartily to his favorite pastime—drinking. And before long he fell sound asleep. The young man, or as you might have guessed, Robin Hood, proceeded to rob the helpless tinker of his purse and the Sheriff's warrant. Then calling the innkeeper, Robin gave him a wink and a smile, and told him that the tinker would pay the whole score when he awoke. Robin departed, leaving the drunken Master Middle in the lurch. When the tinker awoke, he found himself robbed of his purse and stuck with a handsome bill from the innkeeper of ten shillings. Since he had no money, he was forced to pay with his hammer, working bag, and even his leathern coat. And that is how Robin met the Sheriff's daughter's tricks with tricks of his own.

Now you must know that over a year passed and the Sheriff still could not stop Robin's band. The merry band numbered one hundred and forty by this time. The Sheriff had kept his job only because King Harry had died, leaving his son Richard as successor, who did not hold the same concern for the outlaws.

Robin had decided to throw himself upon the mercy of the new King and swear allegiance, but before he could do so, King Richard left on a crusade to the Holy Land, leaving his cruel brother, Prince John in charge.

The Sheriff, hearing that King Richard had left the country, did a very foolish thing. He went to London town believing the Prince would aid him against Robin. The outlaw's power was growing throughout the land, and the Sheriff hoped he could get more troops from the Prince to battle Robin's band. But Prince John heard his plea with nothing but scorn.

"Pooh!" said the Prince, shrugging his shoulders. "What have I to do with all this? Go, get thee gone, and devise thy own tricks to catch the rebel. Never let me see thy face at court again until thou hast a better tale to tell."

So away the Sheriff went like a whipped puppy back to Nottingham. All along the way, he tried to think of a plan to capture Robin Hood and save his job in the bargain.

His daughter met him on his return and saw at once that he had failed. But just as she was about to scold him for going to see the Prince, a wicked idea came to her.

"I have it!" she exclaimed with a cry. "Why should we not hold another shooting-match? It is Fair year, as you know, and another tourney will be expected. Now we will proclaim a general amnesty, as did King Harry himself, and say that the field is open and unmolested to all comers. And you know well Robin and his men will be unable to resist showing off their skill, and then—"

"And then," said the Sheriff jumping up and rubbing his hands with delight, "we shall see on which side of the gate they stop over-night! I will have Robin Hood yet! Ah, my daughter, so clever—you are indeed the apple of your father's eye, my child."

When news of the upcoming contest reached Robin, there was no holding him back. His men warned against a trap, but Robin would hear none of it. Little John suggested they lay aside their suits of Lincoln green and each wear a garment of a different color. All agreed, and when the day of the tourney arrived, Robin's entire company passed through the town gates unharmed.

The competition began, and though all who shot that day had excellent marks, it was Robin that claimed the highest honors. Even with the disguise the Sheriff knew that only the outlaw could shoot so fair, and decided to seize Robin when he presented the prize.

The Sheriff grabbed hold of Robin as the prize arrow was presented, but received for his effort a side blow from the fist of Little John. Fighting broke out everywhere and the crowd

was sent scurrying for safety.

The battle was fierce and many men took fresh cuts. As Robin was fighting, he heard Little John bellow—and saw an arrow had struck his friend in the knee. Coming to his friend's aid, Little John begged Robin to kill him before the Sheriff's men laid hands upon him. But Robin paid no heed and set the big man across his shoulders. The gallant men fought off the soldiers as Robin carried his injured friend to the safety of the forest.

But all was not well, as Robin soon found, for in the fight Will Stutely had been captured and Maid Marion was missing. The next day, as the Sheriff was sitting down to breakfast, he received a message carried on a speeding arrow crashing through his window. It was the prize from the fair. The note read:

"This from one who will take no gifts from liars; and who henceforth will show no mercy. Look well to yourself. R.H."

The following day the Sheriff set guards everywhere around the town square and barred entry, for he was determined to hang Will Stutely at noon. Robin and his men gathered in the woods just outside town to prepare a rescue. A palmer, often known as beggar priests, approached Much the miller's son and told him that the town gate could not be passed. They must enter through the back gate and fight their way to the gallows. While Robin and his men moved behind the town, Much and the hooded palmer entered the front gate unchallenged. The palmer asked the Sheriff if he might give the prisoner his last rites and he reluctantly agreed. But as the palmer spoke to Will, he suddenly cut the noose away and Robin's men flooded in from all sides to join the battle.

As the fighting raged, Robin saw the palmer was in dire need of assistance and quickly came to his side. But as they fought together the palmer's hood fell back, revealing the face of Maid Marion.

"Marion!" cried Robin, "you here!"

"I had to help, Robin," she said simply, " I knew you would not let be come otherwise."

Robin and his band would not have escaped the Sheriff's

men if a good knight, Sir Richard of Lea, a long-time friend, had not intervened. The knight and his men stood before the soldiers and held them till the outlaws made good their escape. During the battle, Robin let fly an arrow that severely wounded the Sheriff, and without a leader, the soldiers soon disbanded and fled.

King Richard had returned from the Holy Land, and Sir Richard of Lea decided he must speak truly to the King of Robin's plight. When the King heard the wild tales of Robin's bold adventures, he decided he must meet this outlaw himself and discover the man's worth.

So it came to pass that on one cold rainy night a stranger appeared at the door of the Friar Tuck's cottage.

"Now by Saint Peter!" growled the friar, "who comes here at this unseemly hour!"

"Ho! Within there! Open, I say!"

"Go your way in peace!" roared back the friar; "I can do nothing for you. The town of Gamewell is not far away, if you know the road."

"But I do not know the road, and if I did I would not budge another foot," replied the stranger. "'Tis wet outside and dry within. So open, without further delay!"

When the friar opened the door he found the figure of a tall knight stood before him.

"Have you no supper, brother?" the knight asked.

"None for you, friend," replied the friar.

"Surely, with the rain and cold about this night you can offer up a meal and bed to a weary fellow?" the knight simply said, and then strode pass the friar and made himself at home.

Normally, the friar would have made a fight with his un-welcome guest, but there was something in the stranger's manner that made him hold his hand. Indeed, it was not long before the two fell into good fellowship and drank many a toast that night to each other's health.

In the morning the friar would not accept any gold for lodging the stranger and asked what aid he could render.

"Can you tell me where I might find the outlaw Robin Hood, for I have a message from the King to deliver to him?" the knight said frankly.

"Aye, though I tend mostly to matters religious, I know of the outlaw's haunts," replied the friar slyly.

And so saying, the two set out into the woods toward Robin's greenwood home. Along the way Robin spied the pair and decided to make some lively sport. Approaching them, Robin came boldly up and cried, "Hold!"

"Who is it bids me hold?" asked the knight quietly. "I am not in the habit of yielding to one man."

"Then here are others to keep me company," said Robin, and the knight soon found himself surrounded by a dozen woodsmen.

"I am here on the King's business," the knight remarked calmly.

"God save the King!" said Robin, doffing his cap loyally, "I am Robin Hood, but I say cursed be the man who denies our liege King's sovereignty!"

"Have a care, fellow!" said the knight, "or you shall curse yourself!"

"Nay, the King has no more devoted subject that I," replied Robin gravely, "I invite you to a greenwood feast that you may see our earnest cheer for His Majesty." Then Robin drew forth his bugle and blew three signal blasts for his band. Soon there came a company of men, all dressed in Lincoln green, with fine new bows in their hands and bright short swords at their belts.

The troop retired to the greenwood and a great feast was soon underway. The knight marveled at what he saw and remarked to himself: "These men of Robin Hood's give more obedience than my fellows give to me."

The knight witnessed great feats of archery and wonderful displays of swordplay as the band parried among themselves. Finally, the friar stood before the knight and challenged him to a bit of sport with wooden staffs.

To the surprise of all, the knight made quick work of the

friar, sending him tumbling face first to the ground. As the band broke out in laughter, Sir Richard rode up and stunned the group by addressing the knight, "I trust Your Majesty has not needed our arms before."

"It is the King!" a cry was raised. And Robin with his men fell reverently upon their knees, as one man.

"Your pardon, sire!" exclaimed Robin Hood. "Pardon for these my men who stand ready to serve you all your days!"

"Rise, you men, and as I know you now to be good and worthy fellows, if you swear to serve your King, a pardon you shall have this day!" proclaimed the King.

"We swear!" came the answering shout of Robin and his men.

"Then I give you all free pardon," said King Richard, "and will speedily put your service to the test. For I love such archers as you have shown yourselves to be. England will not produce your like again, for many a day. But I cannot allow you to roam in the forest and shoot my dear; nor to take the law of the land into your own hands. Therefore, I now appoint you to be Royal Archers and mine own special body-guard."

All gratefully sworn their allegiance and the company set off for the Royal Court in London. There each man of Robin's band was given a royal position; some as Royal Archers, others as Head Foresters. Little John was given the title of Sheriff of Nottingham and the former Sheriff was quickly banned. Will Scarlet was given charge of his father's estate that Prince John had seized, with the promise of knighthood. And Will Stutely was made Chief of the Royal Archers.

For Robin Hood, the King bestowed upon him his father's former title, as Earl of Huntingdon, saying: "Come forward, Robin Fitzooth, Earl of Huntingdon," which brought a mighty cheer from the woodsmen. Kneeling before the King, Robin accepted knighthood as Richard drew his sword and touched the former outlaw upon his shoulder.

Then the King proclaimed: "As my first command to you, my lord Earl of Huntingdon, I entreat you to marry the fair Mistress Marion without delay."

"May I obey all Your Majesty's commands as willingly!" cried the Earl of Huntingdon, drawing Marion close by his side. "The ceremony shall take place as soon as we return to Nottingham, if that is, Maid Marion is willing." Marion turned and answered Robin with a kiss.

"Ha! She makes little protest," said the King; "so I shall even give away the bride myself!"

In the morning the company rose early and set off to Nottingham. It was a goodly group. First rode King Richard of the Lion Heart, with his tall figure set forth by the black armor and waving plume in his helm. Then came Sir Richard of the Lea with fourscore knights and men-at-arms. And after them Robin Hood and Maid Marion followed on milk-white steeds. No sooner did they arrive in Nottingham, then a cry went up: "The King is here! The King is here, and hath taken Robin Hood!"

The Sheriff was at first pleased, but soon discovered the full meaning of the King's visit.

"Sir Sheriff," the King began, "I have come to rid the land of outlaws, according to my promise. There be none left, for all have now taken service with their King. And lest there should be further outbreak, I have decided to place Master Little John, a man who fears no other, in the position of Sheriff of Nottingham. You will turn over your keys at once."

The Sheriff bowed, and dared not utter a word.

"And you, my lord Bishop," the King said, turning to the Bishop of Hereford, "the stench of your evil actions has reached my nostrils. We shall demand strict accounting for seized land and acts of cruelty which ill becomes a man of God. But of these matters, we shall attend to later. For now, you shall prepare for a wedding of two of our company at Nottingham Church."

The Bishop also bowed, and then hurried off, glad to escape the King's judgement for the time.

So a lavish wedding took place and news of Robin's favor from the King spread throughout England. And thus, amid feasting and rejoicing, Robin Hood, the new Earl of Huntingdon, and his bride began their wedded life.

Now by good rights this tale should end here, with Robin and Marion living happily ever after, but alas, unpleasant days later befell the lovers and their misfortune as well as their joy must be told. Though many noble deeds were done by Robin and his men in the years that followed, the days of King Richard of the Lion Heart came to an end, and with his death, Prince John took the throne. Prince John imprisoned Robin, but after a few weeks Will Stutely managed his release, and once again the band gathered in the greenwood. They lived quietly in the woodland, but happy times did not return. Finally, under force of King John, Robin and Marion fled to Europe for safety. But within three years Robin lost his beloved wife Marion to the plague, and heartbroken, he returned to Sherwood Forest.

But on the journey Robin grew ill and had to seek aid at a convent near the greenwood.

No one can be sure what befell Robin within those walls, but a nun bled him to cure the sickness, and in doing so, drew too much of the outlaw's blood. Some say it was an accident, but other's believe it was the Sheriff's daughter taking her revenge at last. Gravely ill, Robin drew his horn and bellowed a blast into the greenwood. And Little John heard his old master's call.

"Lift me up, good Little John," Robin said, "and open yon window. Where this arrow shall fall—let them dig my grave." He let the arrow fly deep into the greenwood and then quietly died in the big arms of Little John.

So ended the life of Robin Hood, but his spirit lives on in the hearts of all men who love freedom and the blessings of chivalry.

For over a decade, Unicorn has been
publishing richly illustrated editions of classic
and contemporary works for children and adults.
To continue this tradition,
WE WOULD LIKE TO KNOW WHAT YOU THINK.

If you would like to send us your suggestions or
obtain a list of our current titles, please write to:
THE UNICORN PUBLISHING HOUSE, INC.
P.O. Box 377
Morris Plains, New Jersey, USA 07950
ATT: Dept CLP

❖❖❖❖❖❖❖